Dealing With Attention Deficit Hyperactivity Disorder

Nishant Baxi

ISBN 978-93-5883-049-1
© Nishant Baxi 2023

Published in India 2023 by Pencil

A brand of

One Point Six Technologies Pvt. Ltd.
Unit no. 26, Ground Floor, Building A1,
Wadala Truck Terminal Road,
Near Post Office, Antop Hill, Mumbai - 400037
E connect@thepencilapp.com
W www.thepencilapp.com

DISCLAIMER: *The opinions expressed in this book are those of the authors and do not purport to reflect the views of the Publisher.*

Author biography

I am an experienced content creator and digital/social media marketing professional with a demonstrated history of working in the publishing industry. Skilled in E-Learning, Market Research, Online Advertising, Management, and Business Development, Content Development.

CONTENTS

What Is ADHD Disorder

Basic Facts about ADHD

ADHD is an acronym that stands for Attention Deficit Hyperactivity Disorder. This condition was formerly known as Attention Deficit Disorder, though the name was modified when it was noted that the affected people were also prone to severe hyperactivity.

ADHD commonly manifests in young children, though most of them carry the traits over into adulthood as well. ADHD is also referred to by some people as the "single-synapse" or the "short attention span" problem.

The reason for this is that ADHD's main characteristics are a marked inability to concentrate on any one thing for very long, accompanied by extremely impulsive behavior where the person doesn't stop to think at all when they get an idea or react to a situation.

One of the most common indicators in young children with ADHD is that they get bored easily. ADHD causes a decrease in the mind's capacity to focus on a single act for very long, so anything repetitive or requiring attention will tax the person's mental endurance far more than it would for a normal person. Kids who avoid homework because it's "boring" or doesn't want to do chores for the same reason often have ADHD.

ADHD also shows up in what parents call the "My child is a living ball of yippee" problem. It has other similar names, most of which are unprintable in polite company, but I'm sure you get the point. Afflicted children constantly fidget, never stop moving, run/climb/crawl/jump everywhere, seem to have boundless energy and undirected curiosity about anything and everything, and are almost always getting into trouble as a result. This is often accompanied by a total lack of discipline and self-control.

While the above factors are present in almost every child ever born in the history of the planet, ADHD is only applicable IF the child doesn't "grow out" of the symptoms. This is the reason why ADHD is referred to as a deficiency type of disorder; because, while children will display these symptoms early on and then mature later in life, learning self-discipline and focus, ADHD-afflicted children will develop much slower in their abilities to mentally focus and think logically. If your child still retains the same symptoms well after everyone else his or her age has "outgrown" it, then it usually indicates ADHD.

ADHD is present in adults as well, though because this disorder doesn't completely stunt a person's mental development, only slows it in certain areas, all adults will have the same symptoms but in a lesser and more controllable fashion.

ADHD is classified as an incurable psychological disorder, though modern methods of therapy are available to help ADHD-afflicted children (and their parents!) cope with the effects. The therapy sessions for the kids are geared toward teaching them to take the boundless energy that often accompanies ADHD and redirects it more constructively. The parental therapy sessions teach the parents how to properly address the ADHD problem and teach their kids discipline. The therapy also helps the parents avoid the nervous breakdowns that usually accompany raising a kid with ADHD...

Even though no cure has been discovered for ADHD, it is generally regarded as a relatively minor and non-fatal disorder (except maybe for cases when parents want to kill their kids out of sheer frustration and annoyance). The fact of the matter is, that any child afflicted with ADHD will eventually learn enough self-control to overcome the biggest of its effects.

However, even in adulthood, these people will still retain some semblance of ADHD, manifesting in various ways like absent-mindedness, fickleness, and impulsive behavior. It has also been shown in studies that the traits of ADHD that carry over into adulthood make these same adults more prone than their peers to more serious psychological afflictions like manic depression or melancholia.

Lastly, on a perverse note, ADHD has been proven to be 100% hereditary. This proves the old lines that your parents used to tell you when you were younger, "Someday, your children will put you through what I'm going through". ADHD can also be triggered in a child whose parents don't have ADHD by various environmental influences like verbal abuse or a mother's ingestion of drugs or alcohol while pregnant.

What are the symptoms of ADHD

Symptoms of ADHD in Layman's Terms

ADHD, or Attention Deficit Hyperactivity Disorder, is a partially neurological, partially psychological problem that crops up in some kids. It's genetically hereditary, but can also be triggered by various social and environmental influences. What ADHD does is that the parts of a child's mind and nervous system that deal with control and focus suffer from a slower growth rate than normal, meaning children afflicted by it will learn self-control and discipline more slowly than their peers. This fact usually leads to its own sets of problems that manifest as symptoms you can watch for to see if your child has ADHD. These are given below in terms that any parent will understand.

The Perpetual Yippee Factor - ADHD-afflicted kids will have boundless energy, screaming and laughing at the top of their lungs and generally being hyperactive pests that skitter around all over the place in an ecstatic state of whoopee. Trying to get them to sit still for more than a minute will lead to their fussing and fidgeting.

I'm Bored Mom! - There are two things that an ADHD-afflicted kid will be unable to do. One, they will be unable to focus on or pay attention to anything for more than a few minutes at a time, and forget things that you tell them mere minutes after you say them. Two, they will avoid repetitive and monotonous acts (like schoolwork, taking a bath, or mowing the lawn) like the plague.

The Plan? What's that? - Kids with ADHD have a very hard time focusing on anything, which also leads to difficulty in arranging their thoughts in a controlled and logical fashion. Trying to teach them anything to do with organization, planning, and forethought is a trial in extreme patience.

Don't You Ever Run Out of Gas? - The hyperactivity part of ADHD is what gets a lot of parents annoyed. Kids love to play, it's natural, but these kids take it to extremes, climbing not just trees, but to the roof if they can get away with it. They'll crawl under stuff, clamber over more stuff, they'll rarely walk - why walk when you can run? It's faster! - And move in leaps and bounds at top speed.

Good Reflexes, Poor Control - one of the few seemingly good things about ADHD is that kids who have it essentially develop quicker reflexes than their peers. However, this is because their nervous systems are wired like cars with really large motors and huge gas tanks, but almost no brakes or steering to speak of. Their motor reflexes will be good; their motor CONTROL, on the other hand, will stink. Given the tendency of ADHD-afflicted kids to be perpetually in motion, this also means that they'll usually be stumbling and falling over (or off) everything.

What Does This Button Do... - another neurological effect of ADHD is boundless curiosity. If your kid has more curiosity than a bag full of cats, pokes his nose into everything, never listens when you tell him to NOT pull the lever on the fire extinguisher, and generally has to be burned, electrocuted, bruised, or mauled before he begins to learn to avoid Bad Stuff, then he's probably got ADHD.

Don't You Ever Stop thinking before acting? - This is what some people refer to as the single synapse problem. Your kid gets it into his head to do something, and he'll immediately do it without even pausing for an instant to consider the (often potentially fatal) consequences of his actions.

Putting it all together - as you can see the above factors all link together. Your kid never stops to think because when you try to teach him discipline he gets bored. He then gets hyperactive as a reaction to boredom, fidgets around until he finds something he's curious about, and decides immediately to run to it at full tilt, generally crashing into things while doing so. You then deliver a scathing lecture that he won't pay attention to because lectures bore him, at which point...

The solution? - Therapy, patience, and antacids.

Lots of the above.

Also, keep three things in mind. One, ADHD eventually fades; it just takes longer to grow out of than for other kids. Two: ADHD does NOT lead to bigger psychological problems; so just let it run its course. Three: ADHD is hereditary, so if you seem to remember your parents telling you "someday" you'll get what's coming to you...

Are There Similar Disorders

Disorders That Share Symptoms with ADHD
ADHD, or Attention Deficit Hyperactivity Disorder, is a relatively harmless neurological and psychological disorder that inhibits the rate at which a child learns to focus his or her attention on a subject matter.

This usually manifests in irritating but "natural" childish behavior, like hyperactivity and getting bored easily, along with other problems like a short attention span and very short memory retention. ADHD is never fatal, and while it has been diagnosed as incurable, it DOES fade over time as the child grows.

It is simply that the child's discipline and focus take longer to develop than they normally would for his or her peers. However, several other mental and physical disorders have symptoms that can easily be shrugged off as ADHD, so parents should keep an eye out for the additional symptoms of these other problems instead of shrugging a child's behavior off as ADHD and "something to grow out of".

Psychological Shock Trauma
Whether due to verbal, physical, or even sexual abuse, a child can exhibit the "spaced out" short attention span often connected to ADHD. This inability to focus, however, will NOT be accompanied by hyperactivity and boundless curiosity and energy. Rather, abused children

will often be withdrawn, shy, and afraid of being touched. In the case of physical abuse, also look for bruises, or monitor if the child tends to stay bundled up in long pants and jackets that may hide constant bruising.

Manic Depression

In its manic phase, a manic depressive will exhibit all the hallmarks of ADHD - a short attention span, an inability to stop moving, poorly thought-out logic, single-synapse reactions, constant happiness or energy, and getting bored easily. However, the depressive side will do a total 180-degree turn and the child will become brooding, grumpy, angry, and withdrawn. These sudden mood swings are the hallmark of manic depression, also known as bipolar disorder.

Thyroid Problems

Thyroid problems lead almost exactly to all the behavioral symptoms of ADHD. The only real indicator of the difference between the two is that thyroid problems will also be accompanied by an irregular physical growth pattern, whether stunted growth or getting too tall/heavy too fast. The hormonal imbalances that accompany thyroid problems cause nerve impulses that lead to ADHD-like behavior.

Anxiety and Stress Disorder

Anxiety and stress tend to lead to a short attention span, "jittery" nerves, and an overabundance of adrenalin in the system which leads to hyperactivity just like ADHD. The best way to differentiate the two is that anxiety and stress are often accompanied by paranoia and fear, whereas a child with ADHD will often be almost fearless (due to a lack of forethought and consideration of any consequences of actions taken).

Substance Abuse

Alcohol, nicotine, and especially illegal drugs can take a heavy toll on a child's body. Each of the three major types of substance abuse has its unique symptoms that parents should familiarize themselves with to be sure that their child just has ADHD and isn't indulging in any bad habits. An addict will exhibit almost all the ADHD symptoms but will have others depending on the type of substance being taken. Common behavioral symptoms to watch out for are aggressive behavior and minor theft from family members (selling things for money to support the habit).

Subtle Seizures

For a variety of reasons, different physical ailments can cause subtle, almost imperceptible seizures in a child. These seizures don't start as major shakes, instead of taking the form of minor trembling that's almost undetectable unless you're watching out for it. These manifest as hyperactivity, clumsiness, and the low attention span that's most commonly taken for ADHD. The symptoms are because seizures affect a person's nervous system, reflexes, and coordination.

Sleep Disorders

Lastly, a child suffering from a sleep disorder like narcolepsy or insomnia will often exhibit the absent-minded lack of attention that it shares as a common symptom with ADHD. However, in ADHD the lack of attention span is accompanied by restless energy and hyperactivity, and these will not be present if your child has a sleeping disorder. Instead, the absent-mindedness will be accompanied by a tendency to be tired, drowsy, and doze off suddenly.

What Causes ADHD

What Causes Attention Deficit Hyperactivity Disorder?

The increasing awareness of the condition known as ADHD or Attention Deficit Hyperactivity Disorder has led to a greater understanding of children and adults who were just once thought of as problems of their families and society.

As we have discussed, these are the children who usually can't cope with school or grownups who can't stick to a job – those who were often blamed to fall out of their lives. Now, society is growing to understand that these people have more serious problems that are caused by a disorder that can be treated. What most people don't understand now is what causes attention deficit order. What people know is that it is a very complicated condition that stems from several different factors.

Before discussing the causes of Attention Deficit Hyperactivity Disorder, it is important to discuss what doesn't cause the condition. Many people are confused by myths that ADHD stems from a myriad of causes that aren't related to the disease. Here are some of those wrong assumptions that have been disputed by years of research about the subject matter.

1. Bad diet – the notion that Attention Deficit Hyperactivity Disorder is caused by sensitivity or allergy to certain types of food, particularly baby food, traces back to

the 70s. However, none of the research in the past decades has supported these claims that certain diets cause ADHD. The

misinformation has been reinforced by the media, which suggested that increased intake of foods like sugar tends to make children impulsive and hyperactive. The claim remains unproven and most research has shown no relationship between the intake of sugar on children's behavior and learning patterns.

2. Excessive Television Viewing – another thing that popularly gets blamed to cause Attention Deficit Hyperactivity Disorder is television. Studies indeed have shown that watching violence on television can increase aggression in children which might be similar to the hyperactivity and impulsiveness of ADHD patients, but such behavior isn't tantamount to ADHD. Research has shown that the amount of time spent watching TV by children with ADHD isn't that different from the TV viewing times of children without the disorder.

3. Hormonal Imbalance – since hormones can indeed affect people's behaviors and moods, some think that Attention Deficit Hyperactivity Disordered is caused by hormonal imbalance. However, there hasn't been any significant correlation between hormone levels and the occurrence of ADHD. Hormones may indeed cause people to be impulsive and out of focus at times but they don't necessarily cause ADHD and its many other symptoms.

4. Balance or Vestibular Problems – the clinicians during the early times of ADHD discovery proposed that the behavior and learning problems stem from the brain's vestibular system, which is responsible for proper balance.

These clinicians proposed that treatment for Attention Deficit Hyperactivity Disorder should involve treatment of motion sickness. However such hasn't been proven throughout the years of research about both ADHD and the vestibular system. So far, none of the research has linked the two with each other.

5. Parenting and Family Life – since the majority of the symptoms of Attention Deficit Hyperactivity Disorder involve behavioral problems, many people blame poor parenting or family problems as the cause of the disorder. Their parents have raised not all children with ADHD poorly and not all children that come from dysfunctional families have ADHD. If a child with ADHD can't be kept still at his or her desk in class, it doesn't mean that his or her parents did not tell him that such is bad behavior. ADHD children may have received adequate discipline from their parents, or perhaps even more, but since their problem also has neurological components, their behavior can still be hard to manage.

Given that all these haven't been proven to cause ADHD, people can now focus on the more plausible causes of Attention Deficit Hyperactivity Disorder. The majority of the factors point to more neurological, genetic, and prenatal factors. Knowing what doesn't cause Attention Deficit Hyperactivity Disorder helps people to know what causes the condition. Up to now, clinicians still haven't come up with a definitive etiology of ADHD. But hopefully, with better research, the mystery of this serious condition may soon be unlocked.

Diagnosing ADHD In Children

Diagnosing Attention Deficit Hyperactivity Disorder in Children

In the past few years, the world has become very interested in Attention Deficit Hyperactivity Disorder. In the past, children who behaved badly in school or failed to perform normally in life were just considered problems in society, assumed to be products of bad parenting, too much television, and other factors. But now, societies are recognizing that such individuals may be afflicted by a condition that is beyond their control. With such a heightened awareness of ADHD, more parents are becoming open to the possibility that their child may have it. As such, it is important to know the process of diagnosing Attention Deficit Hyperactivity Disorder in children.

With such a wide resource of information about Attention Deficit Hyperactivity Disorder, it is very tempting to overdiagnose the disorder. It would be rare to find anyone who has never experienced an episode of inattentiveness, impulsivity, and other symptoms that are similar to those experienced by ADHD patients.

However, it is very dangerous to base diagnoses on merely reading about them. It is just like how medical students, after reading about different types of diseases, suddenly fear that they might have contracted anything from leprosy to tuberculosis. ADHD is a serious condition and one that needs experts for careful examination and diagnosis. Children have to undergo a long process before being declared to have ADHD.

Pre-Diagnosis

While the formal diagnosis of ADHD is done in the clinic, the crucial identification of Attention Deficit Hyperactivity Disorder may begin at home or in school. This happens upon the emergence of suspicion on the part of the parent or the teacher that something different may be happening with a child.

The detection of probable symptoms of ADHD happens usually in school because this is where a child that may have the condition can be singled out from the rest of the kids. Parents, especially first-timers, who don't have a benchmark of normal behavior might not be able to notice the symptoms of ADHD as much as a teacher who sees a bunch of kids every day. And as such, detection is usually done in school.

Evaluation

Once a child is suspected of having Attention Deficit Hyperactivity Disorder, the parents are suggested to have their child evaluated by their family doctor or a specialist diagnostician.

The preliminary evaluation normally involves an interview and observation of the child. At this stage, the practitioner thoroughly investigates the child's medical history as well as the family. A physical check-up is also performed along with interviews with the child, the parents, and the teacher or teachers. The parents and the teachers also observe and rate the child's behavior. Some psychological tests are also given to the child to measure the IQ, emotional and social adjustment, and to identify the presence of learning disabilities. There shouldn't be any medical tests such as brain scans and X-rays at this point unless the practitioner suspects other problems.

Diagnosing Proper

Once the diagnostician gathers all the important data, he or she will then determine whether the child indeed has Attention Deficit Hyperactivity Disorder, the child that doesn't have ADHD might have other problems, or the child has another disorder coexisting with ADHD.

To come up with the first determination, the diagnostician matches the findings with the criteria set by the DSM-IV, the Diagnostic and Statistical Manual of Mental Disorders of the American Psychiatric Association. According to the manual, there should be at least six manifestations of inattentiveness or hyperactivity and impulsivity occurring within six months to degrees of being maladaptive or disruptive. These manifestations should also occur in at least two settings such as at home or in school. The signs should cause serious impairment in the patient's functioning. These signs shouldn't just be parts of other conditions like anxiety or mood disorders.

The second determination is made when the findings don't match the criteria set by the DSM for ADHD, but instead match the criteria for other disorders such as Schizophrenia, Dissociative Disorder, Anxiety Disorder, Mood Disorder, etc. The third determination is only made if the first determination has been set and other problems exist with the presence of another condition co-existing with ADHD.

Diagnosing Attention Deficit Hyperactivity Disorder in Children is indeed a very serious and long process. There are no shortcuts to do it to make sure that all diagnoses are accurate as possible.

Diagnosing ADHD In Adults

Diagnosing Attention Deficit Hyperactivity Disorder in Adults

Many adults have Attention Deficit Hyperactivity Disorder who aren't even aware that they have the condition. Most of them have just learned through time how to adjust to their bouts of inattention, disorganization, distractibility, incorrigible tardiness, and inability to keep stable jobs.

Others have just resolved that they are incapable of keeping focus and no longer bother seeking help or instilling change on their own. Sadly, these people don't know that such are signs of a disorder that can be treated through medical and psychological intervention. That is why diagnosing Attention Deficit Hyperactivity Disorder is an important issue to address.

The procedure involved in diagnosing Attention Deficit Hyperactivity Disorder is somewhat similar to the process done in children since childhood and adult ADHD are very much related.

However, there are big differences between diagnosing children and adults, obviously because of the different age groups and contexts. There is a great advantage in the diagnostic process with more mature individuals since they have more of their insights and they are more capable of giving out their observations about themselves.

The danger, however, is that many adults may overanalyze observations and link them immediately to the symptoms they have heard about. Conversely, some adults may try to conceal important information out of embarrassment or self-preservation. The diagnosis of ADHD in adults is thus as complicated as the diagnosis of the condition in children.

The diagnostic process for adults with ADHD usually begins with individuals or peers. Unlike children who need parents or teachers to notice something different about their behavior, adults are more capable of seeing if there might be something wrong with the way their lives function. This usually happens about the time the adult becomes independent and notices how hard it is to cope with work or school (usually in the university) compared to other people in his or her environment.

There are also times when colleagues and friends are the ones who notice some peculiarities in a particular individual. When the differences seem to pose impairments in the life of the individual, it is then that the intervention of an expert is called for. Either the individual himself should seek the help of a professional or the colleagues will suggest the need for professional help.

The diagnostic process itself begins when the adult who suspects he has ADHD, approaches a health practitioner to have himself examined. The preliminary assessment is usually done in the clinic beginning with an extensive diagnostic interview. A thorough investigation of the patient's history is done by digging into the development as a child, health history, school records, job history, history of social relationships, behavior patterns throughout childhood and adolescence, drug or alcohol history, and history of the psychiatric profile.

The completeness of the interview is crucial in diagnosing Attention Deficit Hyperactivity Disorder accurately. The patient must be completely honest during the interview so that the practitioner will be able to gather all the important information for diagnosis.

After the clinical assessment interview, the adult suspecting ADHD will be given a battery of tests to assess the neuropsychological profile. The battery of tests will measure the individual's academic achievement, intellectual functioning, memory, attention span, and other processes that may be affected by ADHD. The patterns of the individual's scores are analyzed to see if they follow the same patterns exhibited by ADHD patients.

While adult ADHD and childhood ADHD are related, there are certain important variations in the symptoms since some behaviors that are very much prevalent during childhood may no longer be present in adulthood, but instead, have developed into a different, yet still related form. The hyperactivity of an ADHD child exemplified by constant running around or climbing during inappropriate times may become restlessness in the ADHD adult. Physical impulsivity of younger ADHD patients may then become verbal impulsivity in their grown-up counterparts. The inattention in the classroom may morph into inattention at work. The diagnostician is then tasked to watch out for these adult forms of ADHD symptoms.

Diagnosing Attention Deficit Hyperactivity Disorder in adults still hasn't been established as much as in children. And thus it is important to consult specialists to come up with accurate diagnoses of the condition.

Education and ADHD Children in Public Schools

Education and ADHD Children in Public Schools

The quick rise of the awareness of Attention Deficit Hyperactivity Disorder is a much-welcomed phenomenon that greatly favors individuals who were once thought to be problem children. Before people were ostracized and blamed for not being able to cope with schoolwork or focus their attention in class and eventually in their jobs.

Now, society is more forgiving and understanding that these individuals may be suffering something that impairs their lives significantly, making it difficult to adjust to important social settings such as school or work.

However, promising as this may sound, it can cause adverse effects on public school students who are now prone to be wrongfully labeled as having ADHD. This is why it is important to discuss education and ADHD children in public schools.

There are two dangers for ADHD children in public schools. The first one is that children can easily be mislabeled as ADHD children for even the minutest signs of misbehavior. The second danger is the exact opposite, children who genuinely have ADHD are not diagnosed as such either to the lack of awareness of the educators or the skepticism about Attention Deficit Hyperactivity Disorder itself as a valid condition.

Both problems can be present in public schools and both are equally detrimental to the proper development of children. It is important to have the right education to nurture children studying in public schools with special needs.

The first problem stems from the increased awareness but lack of understanding of ADHD on the part of the teachers. Indeed it is good that more people, especially teachers, are becoming aware of ADHD – that it is a valid condition that can afflict children and affect their behavior in school and hinder them from coping with academic requirements.

However, for the most part, the awareness isn't tantamount to a deep understanding of the disorder. Teachers in public schools that lack resources for proper diagnostics of ADHD can dangerously label children exhibiting some misbehavior to be ADHD patients. The hazard of this is tremendous. The child may unnecessarily be given the stigma of ADHD patients, or worse the child could be subjected to unnecessary procedures that may affect his or her self-esteem.

The second problem poses an equally devastating scenario that can indeed be detrimental to the child as well. Children who may genuinely have attention deficit hyperactivity disorder may instead be labeled as plain old troublemakers that deserve to be disciplined instead of being given proper treatment. They are those children that are left out of activities or made to sit at the back of the classroom for not being able to keep them in a behavior that is considered to be proper.

What is sad is that not only do these children become deprived of treatment for their condition but they are also dealt with contempt or even condemnation. Their conditions are worsened by the fact that their learning impairments are exacerbated by their self-esteem even becoming lower as they are marginalized in their schools.

Another disadvantage that is usually present among public schools is the greater number of students and the larger class sizes. This prevents ADHD children from getting enough attention from their educators. It is difficult enough for teachers to manage a large class; it is even problematic to manage children with ADHD and possibly some learning disabilities.

ADHD children, along with children who have learning disabilities, need special attention and education. This is usually difficult to achieve in most public schools except for those that are equipped with the proper resources to address the concerns of kids with special needs.

The need to address the needs of children with special educational requirements can't be overstressed. The advocacy to equip public schools with more resources to be able to educate ADHD should be pushed forward to give ADHD children the chance to move up the ranks of society and function as well as they can. ADHD shouldn't be a hindrance to the success of these children, especially now that more ways of coping with the condition have been developed.

Education for **ADHD** Children in the Private Sector

Education for ADHD Children in the Private Sector

It is quite a relief to know that the world is growing much more aware of the issue of Attention Deficit Hyper Activity Disorder and the way the condition can greatly affect the lives of its sufferers, particularly children in school. In the past, a child who was unable to focus in school was impulsive, and fidgety was labeled as a problem child that wouldn't be able to succeed in life.

Nowadays, people recognize that such children might be suffering from a valid condition that can be treated and managed with various options available nowadays. While this is indeed a promising thought, it is still saddening that the understanding of ADHD is rather shallow, particularly in public schools, where resources for ADHD children might be below. Such is why a lot of parents seek alternative Education for ADHD children in the private sector.

It isn't uncommon for ADHD children to experience difficulties in academics and these appear to stem from two serious causes. The primary cause for academic difficulties is the fact that ADHD children find it harder to learn due to their propensity to be distracted, difficulty in finishing tasks, inclination to do things hastily, and difficulty in disciplining themselves.

The second cause is that ADHD might be accompanied by other learning disabilities specific to particular developmental markers such as reading, comprehension, and verbal and written expression, among many others. To cope with the demands of academic life, these two problems have to be addressed whether the child gets an education from the public or the private sector.

The first problem can usually be addressed with medication together with psychological intervention. ADHD is pretty much a neurological disorder as much as a psychological one, which is why an important part of effective treatment is medication.

For a lot of ADHD children, many of the primary symptoms such as inattentiveness and impulsivity are significantly diminished, if not eliminated once they undergo medical treatment. This is greatly beneficial for them as their lives become more conducive to learning since they are more able to focus and become disciplined with schoolwork.

However, it gets problematic if the ADHD child has other problems, especially learning disabilities. If this is the case, the symptoms of ADHD might disappear but the child will still have difficulties in school.

This problem is usually most prevalent among ADHD children in public schools where the resources aren't available and the class sizes are bigger. While with proper medical treatment, ADHD children might gain focusing abilities; they will still need to have special education if they have learning disabilities. Such disabilities can't be treated by medication. Only a good educational program will be able to help children learn with these difficulties.

Usually, only schools in the private sector, especially those that specialize in progressive educational techniques, can offer this. At this point, it is usually only then that ADHD children can receive the ample education they need to cope with academics despite their difficulties.

One great advantage of a lot of private schools is that they can offer smaller class sizes. This is very useful, especially for children who need special attention that can only be given to them if their teachers don't have too large of a class as they usually do in public schools. With such a setting, ADHD children with other learning disabilities can get more assistance throughout their education. A smaller class setting may also help an ADHD child cope if he or she is left behind by the rest of his or her peers. The major disadvantage, however of education in the private sector is the great cost it entails.

Public schools are of course free while private schools aren't. To take advantage of private education parents will have to shoulder considerable costs, and thus it is only available to those who can afford them.

Education for ADHD children is a very serious matter whether it involves the public or private sector. The decision of whether to enter an ADHD child into a private or a public school is indeed one that needs careful consideration, especially since the child's future can greatly depend on his or her education.

A Good IDEA

How the IDEA Law Works, and Why You Should Understand It

Children with disabilities deserve education: they, too, can be productive members of society, if they are given the chance to learn according to their level. Thanks to the Individuals with Disabilities Education Act, or IDEA, children with disabilities don't need to contend with social stigmas or suffer and go unnoticed. They can receive not only quality education but also recognition of their own special needs. If properly implemented, the Individuals with Disabilities Education Act will entail adjustments in the way buildings are designed, restaurants serve customers, and even how websites appear or are designed.

The IDEA has been around for a long while but was amended in 2004 to update the federal law according to the trends of the times. According to the Individuals with Disabilities Education Act, all people with disabilities must receive "a free, appropriate public education." Such an agenda should operate within the disabled person's Individualized Education Program, or IEP, which, is concerned with the person's needs in the Least Restrictive Environment.

That is, public schools must have the capacity to teach children with disabilities, and must therefore have all the instruments to do so. Learning instruments will include learning aids fashioned specifically for children with disabilities, modifications on standardized tests to fit the learning level or test-taking capacity of children with disabilities, and changes to educational institutions in terms of their working area, access from the street, and so on.

The key to the proper exercise of the law is to understand what the IDEA defines as children with disabilities. According to the Individuals with Disabilities Education Act, a child with disabilities may suffer from mental retardation, impairment in speech or language, impairment in hearing (or deafness altogether), impairment in visual skills (or blindness altogether), emotional disturbance of a serious nature, orthopedic or movement-related impairment, brain injury or trauma to the brain, autism, other impairments to health, or learning disabilities. The IDEA further establishes its underlying principles by stating that such children will have special education needs and other related services.

Another important element of the Individuals with Disabilities Education Act is the establishment of the Individualized Education Program, which is fashioned specifically for the child with disabilities if the child is found to be eligible for the IDEA.

The Program is designed by specialists, which, according to the law, should include a general education teacher, a school psychologist or standardized testing specialist, a school administrator, a teacher skilled in special education should the child require a special education program, and the child's parents. The program should also include goals, as well as benchmarks to track the child's progress.

The IDEA also requires that all children with disabilities should receive education from pre-school to secondary school, along with services related to education, all at no cost to the child's guardians or parents. There will be fees imposed, however, for services related to the care of disabled toddlers or infants. A public school district is also tasked to identify which students have what disabilities, and whether or not such students are attending public schools.

The Least Restrictive Environment requirement of IDEA simply states that children with disabilities shouldn't be isolated from children their age unless the disability is severe or education is impossible for the disabled child if he or she is placed in a regular classroom. The Least Restrictive Environment refers not only to the classroom or location in which the disabled child is placed but also to the method used in teaching the child. In other words, the IDEA hopes to make children with disabilities feel that they truly are part of society as early as elementary school.

Another issue relevant to parents is the discipline of a child with disabilities. According to the Act, a child with disabilities should be disciplined only if the disability is first taken into context. For instance, some children with disabilities may be agitated by loud noises, and shouldn't be spanked or scolded if they run out of noisy classrooms or stay away from playgrounds. If a child with disabilities has accumulated ten or more days in a year of faulty conduct in his or her school, the child's situation may be assessed and a hearing may be conducted.

If you have a child with disabilities and are interested in details about the Individuals with Disabilities Act, contact your local government. Read as much as you can about the IDEA at your local library. This law is for parents like you who dream about having a better world for their children, no matter what disabilities their children have.

Pharmaceutical Treatments for ADHD

What are the Pharmaceutical Treatments for ADHD?

At the risk of sounding repetitive Attention-Deficit/Hyperactivity Disorder, commonly referred to as ADHD, is a disorder characterized by long, frequent periods of inattention, as well as hyperactivity or impulsivity. The disorder, which may stem from an underlying surplus or deficiency in certain molecules in the body, can appear in early childhood. Children with ADHD will often be forgetful, have poor control over their impulses, will be easily distracted, and can sometimes be disruptive.

This disease has no medical cure yet, although there are several pharmaceutical treatments available that target certain aspects of the disease, all of them with the hope of easing the disease without making it disappear altogether. Because of the recent influx of research on the disease, diagnosis of it is easier, and more and more adults are found to suffer from it.

Research shows that ADHD can be inherited, although about twenty percent of ADHD cases are the result of brain injury in the womb, perhaps due to ingestion of toxins or physical trauma to the infant.

ADHD pharmaceutical treatments consist of taking stimulant medication which can be combined with changes in a child's lifestyle, modification of the child's behavior, and continuous counseling. If you or your child is suffering from ADHD, you will need to consult with a doctor on what medications are best suited for your case. You will also need to monitor your or your child's progress constantly to check the medication's effectiveness.

One such medication is Adderall, which is used to treat both narcolepsy and ADHD. Adderall increases a child's attention and can decrease restlessness, and is given only with a prescription. Side effects may include dizziness, diarrhea, increased heart rate, decreased appetite, tics, increased blood pressure, headaches, insomnia, decreased weight, constipation or cramps, dry mouth, impotence, and depression.

Adderall may also interfere with the activity of certain antihistamines, glutamic acid, blood pressure medications, tranquilizers, seizure medications, and antidepressants. High-acidity food products, such as those containing Vitamin C or citrus juices can also keep the body from absorbing Adderall.

Bupropion hydrochloride is often marketed under the brand name Wellbutrin, Wellbutrin SR, or Zyban. It is used to treat ADHD and depression and is as effective as the most common medication, Ritalin. Like Adderall, bupropion hydrochloride can't be bought without a prescription and should be used in conjunction with other treatment methods such as counseling and special education. The most common side effects of taking this medication include agitation, nausea, lower appetite, decreased weight, confusion, seizures, and insomnia. Bupropion hydrochloride may also cause seizures, especially if it is taken with alcohol.

Catapres and Dixarit both fall under the generic Clonidine, which can be used to treat blood pressure aside from ADHD. Side effects can include dizziness, constipation, decreased appetite, dry eyes, fatigue, drowsiness, and headaches. Clonidine can also interfere with the action of antidepressants, beta-blockers, and cough or cold medicines. Taking Clonidine may also require you to have your blood pressure and weight checked regularly.

Dextroamphetamine is commonly marketed under the brand name Dexedrine, and, like Adderall, is used to treat both narcolepsy and ADHD by increasing attention and decreasing restlessness. Like Adderall, Dextroamphetamine can also cause nausea, dry mouth, nervousness, dizziness, increased heart rate, changes in mood, cramps or constipation, decreased appetite, headaches, and insomnia. You will also need to consult with your doctor if you are taking decongestants, glutamic acid, blood pressure medication, or seizure medications along with dextroamphetamine.

Cylert is the brand name of the generic Pemoline, which is used to treat both ADHD and narcolepsy by stimulating the central nervous system. Cylert can cause weight loss, abdominal pain, changes in mood, tics, decreased appetite, insomnia, drowsiness, nausea, and impaired motor coordination.

Because some disorders can have the same manifestations as ADHD, a conclusive diagnosis must first be made before Cylert is prescribed. Cylert, moreover, can cause liver damage, which can manifest in darkened urine, fatigue, jaundice, and abdominal pain.

Strattera, a non-stimulant medication, can be used to treat ADHD and is therefore not a controlled substance.

Although the trade of Strattera isn't relatively strictly regulated, it can still cause side effects such as vomiting, lower appetite, fatigue, nausea, abdominal pains, dizziness, painful urination, and dry mouth.

Ritalin, Concerta, and Metadate are the most popular medications for ADHD and fall under the generic name methylphenidate. These medications stimulate the central nervous system, which can increase attention and decrease restlessness. Methylphenidate can also cause stomach pains, decreased appetite, insomnia, rapid heart rate, slow growth, dizziness, vision changes, and drowsiness. Methylphenidate may also interfere with diet pills, amphetamines, asthma or cold medication, and other ADHD medications such as Cylert.

In the next chapter, we will take a more in-depth look at some of these medications and how they are considered in the medical community.

Controversy in the Medical Community

Medications for ADHD: Why They're Causing a Stir

There are quite a several controversies in the medical arena, but none of them are so loaded with implications as those surrounding attention-deficit/hyperactivity disorder, or ADHD. Until recently, children who were noisy or disruptive were either considered to be difficult to discipline, and thus merited no attention; or were the products of parents who didn't know how to raise their children, and were thus to be pitied. When a child couldn't pay attention in school, he or she was labeled as a slow learner and was often looked down upon by his or her peers.

As we have discussed, today, such behavior can be diagnosed as a manifestation of ADHD. ADHD-affected children will be impulsive, easily distracted, hyperactive, forgetful, and disruptive. This chronic condition persists into adulthood; and, owing to the increasing volume of research conducted in the field, more adults are being diagnosed with ADHD. ADHD has also been shown to be a hereditary disorder, with about a fifth of all cases found to be the result of a brain injury, either chemical or physical, to the child in the womb.

The controversy surrounding ADHD stems from the diagnosis itself. Some parents and psychologists contend that the behavioral manifestations of ADHD are simply normal childhood behavior that can get out of control because of poor upbringing. Therefore, they recommend that children who have been "diagnosed" with ADHD not be given medication, but should instead be counseled and controlled. Another school of thought on the matter regards ADHD as a real disorder, and thus maintains that pharmaceutical medication is continued, as it can ease the symptoms of the disease.

There is no way to treat ADHD permanently, and those who suffer from it have to take medication all their lives. Such an arrangement begs many different questions, primarily where safety is concerned. As you now know, there are different medications for ADHD, with some of them initially used to treat narcolepsy by targeting certain parts of the nervous system.

As we discussed in the previous chapter such medications, which include the popular Ritalin and Concerta, can have dire side effects, such as the increased risk of stroke, increased blood pressure, increased heart rate or severe palpitations, arrhythmia, and irregular heart rhythm.

The United States Food and Drug Administration, or USFDA, has long studied the effects of ADHD drugs and has stamped them with a black box warning. That is, such drugs are regulated and can be prescribed, but strong caution must be exercised when such drugs are taken. In addition to FDA studies, another advisory panel has evaluated evidence pointing to long-term psychiatric changes and cardiovascular risks in children who take ADHD medication. The panel found that such drugs could increase the risk of mania, psychosis, aggressive behavior, and hallucinations in children suffering from ADHD.

Such findings have caused controversy around the use of these drugs, although psychiatrists caution people about making literal interpretations of these findings. According to the documents submitted to the second evaluating panel, the risk of psychiatric diseases being worsened because of ADHD medication was very small; and many cardiovascular diseases, such as higher blood pressure, arose because of existing heart-related conditions in persons suffering from ADHD.

Despite these risks, psychiatrists and doctors continue to recommend ADHD medications, especially since such medications have so far proven to be safe. There is a good deal of literature and research available tackling ADHD medications – and much more than a good number of other medications that have long been approved and are currently being prescribed. The key to maintaining safety is to closely and regularly monitor ADHD patients while these medications are being administered. For instance, some medications can hamper growth in young children, so children suffering from ADHD have to be regularly weighed and measured while they are taking such ADHD medications.

Since ADHD medication can sometimes induce hallucinations, some parents worry about long-term effects or addiction in children with ADHD. Studies have shown, however, that stopping medication can also stop hallucinations. Nevertheless, a physician has to be the one to dictate when medication should be stopped, and parents are cautioned against changing medications on their own or making up their regimens.

Moreover, treatment of ADHD doesn't end with ADHD medication. All medication must be used together with treatment regimens such as counseling, special education, and behavior modification. If you or your child is suffering from ADHD, then consult with your doctor regularly on what treatment and medication options, and obligations are available to you. Do as much research as you possibly can on these treatments and medication regimens, and be aware of all the side effects, advantages, and disadvantages associated with them. As long as you are well informed about ADHD, you can't go wrong.

Natural Remedies for ADHD

Going Back to Basics: Natural Remedies for ADHD

In the past, rowdy, disruptive children were often spanked or scolded, while their parents were looked upon with disdain. With increasing research on child behavior, as well as with more studies on how molecular imbalances can trigger certain kinds of behavior and movements, physicians and psychiatrists have found that such unfortunate parents and noisy children should be treated with consideration.

As you know from reading thus far, they have given a name to such a phenomenon: Attention-Deficit/Hyperactivity Disorder (ADHD).

ADHD now considered a developmental disorder, is caused by changes in brain molecule levels, which in turn can be caused by head trauma in the womb. This head or brain trauma may be physical in nature, or chemical, say if the expectant mother ingested certain toxins.

Children with ADHD tend to be impulsive and forgetful. They are also hyperactive and easily distracted. Because the disorder persists into adulthood, more and more adults are finding that their distractibility is due to ADHD.

ADHD also has a strong genetic component, and can thus be inherited. ADHD can't be cured, and its symptoms can be eased only with a combination of behavioral modification, special education, parental support, lifestyle changes in the person suffering from the disorder, and special medications meant to target the central nervous system. Popular ADHD medications have been used to treat blood pressure disorders and narcolepsy, and they can include the popular Ritalin, Cylert, and Strattera.

After reading about these medications and reviewing opposing points of view amongst the medical and psychiatric communities, you must consider the consequences of taking ADHD medications in the long term even though it hasn't been thoroughly studied.

Many ADHD medications also have dangerous side effects. In general, they can cause nausea, vomiting, abdominal pains, constipation, cramps, insomnia, and depression. In extreme cases, some ADHD medications have exacerbated existing cardiovascular disorders, such as high blood pressure and heart conditions; or have worsened certain psychiatric disorders such as mania and psychosis.

There is another component to consider. That is ADHD medications work by increasing alertness and attention, and by decreasing restlessness. Because of these properties, people who don't suffer from ADHD can and do abuse the drug. For instance, some students believe that ADHD medications can make them perform better in school by focusing their attention.

The disorder itself is subject to controversy. Some psychiatrists and parents contend that the symptoms of ADHD can be surmounted and obliterated by the proper discipline; in some extremes, some people don't consider ADHD a disorder at all. Backed by scientific proof, however, other scientists and physicians believe that ADHD is a real disorder that can be eased, thanks to long-term medication.

Long-term medication, however, doesn't sit well with many people. Some psychiatrists, physicians, and even parents of ADHD-affected children cite their positive experiences with holistic medicine and natural ADHD medications. Before using such medications or even recommending them, however, you must read as much as you can on what advantages and disadvantages they carry. Moreover, you should always consult with your physician on what options are available to you before plunging into any natural or holistic treatments.

There are many natural treatment regimens available for ADHD, but the most common so far is a change in diet. ADHD-friendly diets are generally free from stimulants, such as sugars and preservatives, all of which can exacerbate ADHD symptoms and even interfere with the effectiveness of ADHD medications. There are many names for such diets, but in summary, they recommend that junk foods be taken out totally. Some junk foods contain a chemical called tartrazine, which is used to color foods and can increase hyperactivity.

Holistic medicine practitioners also recommend certain drinks to help calm adults suffering from ADHD. Instead of taking ADHD medications, adults are asked to take yoga classes, which can help them concentrate, as well as monitor their breathing patterns. Adults suffering from ADHD are also requested to drink calming beverages, such as chamomile tea, instead of relying on ADHD medications to calm them down.

Holistic medicine practitioners also recommend certain herbs that can be integrated into an ADHD-friendly diet. For instance, fresh lemon balm can induce calm; while ginkgo Biloba tablets can increase concentration. Melatonin can also regulate the body's sleep cycles and induce relaxation while Saint John's Wort can ease depression without pushing the body into hyperactivity. People with ADHD are also encouraged to take vitamins to increase concentration. Such vitamins can include Vitamin B complex, Vitamin C, and Zinc.

Other techniques, such as massage, magnet therapy, and even acupuncture have been used to calm people with ADHD and regulate their body cycles. These are only a few natural techniques that you may want to consider if you are looking for ways to cure ADHD. Always be on the alert for new research in the field of ADHD treatment, and be sure that you thoroughly and truly understand the underlying principles governing the use of your natural treatment of choice before you or your child use it to combat ADHD.

Alternative Treatments for ADHD

Alternative Treatments for ADHD: Are They Safe? Do They Work?

Alternative treatments have always existed alongside the more conventional treatments, often to supplement and sometimes, to substitute. While some alternative treatments have shown some promise to people with ADHD, many of them are considered unsafe and some have unproven effects. Positive results from some alternative treatments are also often dismissed as akin to the placebo effect, especially since these treatments and therapies haven't undergone rigorous scientific study and testing.

However, alternative treatments remain serious contenders for treating ADHD. Many people who have family members with ADHD often turn to alternative treatments either out of exhaustion from the stress associated with the disorder or from sheer hope that maybe, this specific treatment just might help. Here, we examine some of the more popular alternative treatments for ADHD and what we can expect:

Nutritional supplementation
Some studies have shown that nutritional supplements may offer benefits for children with ADHD. However,

this shouldn't be misconstrued as a sign that ADHD is a result of malnutrition. After all, the diets of children with ADHD aren't much different from those who don't have the disorder.

The argument for mega-vitamins and supplements to treat ADHD is that many of the mental disorders we know are often caused by nutritional deficiencies. As such, proponents of mega-vitamins for ADHD insist that this approach may hold water.

The only hurdle that stands in the way of this premise is that the evidence that accompanies this argument is modest at best. Whatever benefits vitamin treatments and therapies provide seem to be limited to certain
groups of individuals with ADHD who happen to have a function-impairing nutritional deficiency. In general treatment for ADHD, mega-vitamins haven't proven much.

Biofeedback

EEG results from people with ADHD are different from those who don't have the disorder. The brain waves of people with ADHD seem to show larger amplitude, a state of the brain that is often associated with daydreaming and sleep. This is when individuals with ADHD are awake.

To treat the 'sleeping brain', a common therapy called EEG Biofeedback Training is used to attempt to change abnormal brain wave patterns and turn them into normal patterns. Biofeedback has been around since the 70s and according to some of its supportive researchers; it can benefit at least 80% of people with ADHD.

Certain studies and current research have also supported the positive effects of EEG biofeedback, with as many as 80% of children treated showing improvements and reducing their medications without regression. However, biofeedback is only limited to helping children improve their social skills and

academic performances and help them gain a certain amount of control over their disorder. It still won't eliminate or cure ADHD.

Homeopathic treatments
A study that was published in 1997 by the British Homeopathic Journal indicated that homeopathic treatments seemed to lessen ADHD symptoms and behavior in children. It stated further that even when stopped, more than half of the children who received homeopathic treatments still improved while 24% suffered from relapse and the rest enjoyed positive results as long as the homeopathic treatments were continued.
Homeopathic treatments are often relied on and trusted because they are used with all-natural medicines. The only problem is that this treatment is also unproven as a solution for ADHD. While many people report positive results from homeopathic treatment, experts agree that it should be considered experimental, since there are no studies that can support its beneficial effects on ADHD.
Other alternative treatments
Numerous other alternative treatments have been used for ADHD. Hypnotherapy, for example, has shown positive results although its effects are limited to children or individuals suffering from tics or sleep problems associated

with ADHD. Other alternative treatments such as sound training, oculovestibular treatment, and vision therapy have also received some attention. Unfortunately, there is no scientific evidence to back up these claims.

More research
Any development related to alternative and innovative treatments shouldn't be automatically opposed or ignored. Looking at possibilities and treatments that may be used beyond the available resources can open doors and lead the way to progress.

The key to ensuring that alternative treatments are used effectively is methodological research. There is a need to ensure that these alternative treatments be evaluated and studied objectively and rigorously. Experimentation and further research will help, although solid funding will do nicely, especially for mental disorders.

As of today, there is no single treatment or therapy that has proven effective for treating ADHD. It is often when two or more treatments are combined that positive results are produced. As for whether or not alternative treatments for ADHD will work, only time and further research will show.

Coping Skills for Patients and Family

Coping Skills for People with ADHD and Their Family
Having a member of the household with ADHD requires a lot of patience and understanding, especially for other family members. If parents or siblings don't understand what ADHD is and are unprepared for it, they may be hurt or annoyed by the patient's behavior. Sometimes, it can also lead to embarrassment and produce enough stress to put a strain on the relationship between the family and their community. In addition to that, there may also be financial concerns associated with children who have ADHD.

Developing coping skills for an ADHD Patient
A child needs to understand his disorder but it's also necessary that he know what his family is doing to help him cope with it. If the patient is a young child, it may be difficult for him or her to cope especially in a social setting like the school or community, where labels such as 'deficient' or 'disorder' or even worse, name-calling may be encountered. This is where support from parents, older siblings, and teachers should play a major part.

For adults with ADHD who may have had bad experiences in their childhood due to the disorder, it's important to keep informed and to seek help if necessary.

By having a thorough understanding of the disorder, it is easier for adults to cope, adapt to a certain lifestyle and maintain their self-esteem.

Coping skills for the family

Usually, parents and siblings of a child who has ADHD don't know about this disorder until after it is diagnosed. Once this diagnosis has been confirmed, the family needs to learn about ADHD and its symptoms to understand it. By knowing the nature of the disorder, it is far easier for other family members to offer understanding and tolerance to an ADHD patient because they know the behaviors aren't done deliberately.

Important coping skills to develop

There is a pattern to the behavior of a child with ADHD. In turn, there is also a pattern to their responses to specific behaviors. Often, the key is in substituting old habits with new ones through hard work and awareness. While this is a lot easier said than done, families will be able to deal with the disorder better and encourage the right behaviors.

It will also help to provide structure for a child with ADHD because this gives a feeling of organization and predictability. Having a set routine will help children with ADHD move within a limited but familiar environment. In case a change is forthcoming, make sure to inform the child (using a countdown is often effective) before introducing something new.

It is also important to develop certain strategies to help cope with the disorder. Learn to break big tasks into smaller ones, for example, or set smaller goals to help you and your child achieve positive results. It is also important to use positive reinforcement instead of harsh discipline as a way to instill good behavior.

Helping other children to cope

Often, having a sibling who has ADHD puts a lot of strain on other children, who will feel hurt or disappointed by their sibling's often aggressive, demanding, or difficult behavior. Since children with ADHD also require more attention, siblings often feel ignored and left out.

If this is a possibility, make sure other children understand what their sibling is going through. Try to spend time talking to other children about their sibling's condition and why they need to give extra attention and

understanding. You might also want to include other siblings (especially older ones) in coming up with coping tips and special arrangements. When children feel they are involved in a family activity, they are more likely to participate and feel responsible for the family member.

Using resources

You can't fight ADHD because you're bound to lose. It also has no known cure so it's important to be able to develop effective coping skills to help manage the disorder and live a healthy life. As such, don't be afraid about using other resources to help ease your struggles and provide you with ways to raise and live with a person with ADHD.

There are numerous books and publications about ADHD that you might want to use for reference. There are also resources on the

The Internet can be a great help in finding coping techniques and learning more about ADHD and other developments. It might also help to join

support groups or get help and advice from professionals and social workers.

Researching ADHD

Between Now and the Future: Researching and Treating ADHD

Attention deficit and hyperactivity disorder or ADHD is still a mystery to many medical experts and professionals. It is a disorder that is often wrongly diagnosed, difficult to understand, and even more
difficult to cope with. Research about this disorder continues today and while new developments have been discovered and promoted, no cure is in sight.

Brain imaging test
A brain-imaging test is part of diagnostic testing for ADHD. Currently, this type of testing can only differentiate between groups of otherwise healthy or normal individuals and people with ADHD. While a brain scan can't detect
the differences between two individuals with the same disorder, it can provide new insights into how ADHD works and what causes it.
However, recent studies involving brain scans of people with ADHD while performing certain tasks proved that they do use certain areas of the brain differently compared to individuals who are otherwise considered normal.

In a study that began at Emory University and is continuing at the University of Maryland, it was found that normal individuals tended to use the verbal sections of the brain while people with ADHD used the visual areas.

This is significant in understanding why it is often difficult for children with ADHD to translate verbal instruction through a visualization process. According to the researcher, this means that people with ADHD have to make the extra effort of visualizing what has just been said instead of using the words and translating them into action.

It was also found that the brains of people with ADHD showed more activity, especially in the motor areas. This might explain why they often exhibit extra movements such as fidgeting. While this study shows a lot of promise for people with ADHD, researchers admit there is still a lot of work and further involvement.

NIMH research

The National Institute of Mental Health has long sponsored and co-sponsored studies and research on many disorders including ADHD. Certain groups of NIMH grantees are involved in studies that hope to determine whether or not there are varieties of ADHD. By finding clusters of symptoms whether they are physical or emotional, scientists hope to be able to develop effective treatments that will target the specific disorders.

The United States Department of Education and the NIMH have agreed to co-sponsor and work together on a nationwide study on ADHD treatments. The study, which will collect data for five years, will tackle the issue of which ADHD treatments work for which type of children with

ADHD. Furthermore, the same study will also examine the efficacy of certain ADHD treatment combinations.

The study also hopes to discover how family status and environmental influences can affect children with ADHD in terms of severity and long-term outcome. The long-term need for ADHD medication and its effect on the the emotional well-being of children will also be included in the study.

When the results of this study are finally gathered, medical professionals and mental health experts hope to be able to determine which different types of medications and/or treatments can offer better results and produce effective outcomes.

Animal research

The use of animal subjects in experiments to further understand the condition of ADHD and to determine the efficacy of certain new treatments is still being conducted.

Animal subjects used during these experiments allow scientists to study certain possible causes of the disorder that may otherwise not be done physically and safely on humans, especially when experiments involve drugs that haven't been used before. For example, one team of researchers and scientists is using dogs to determine how a new, Ritalin-like stimulant can affect the brain.

Pieces of the puzzle

Scientists and medical experts agree that the research on ADHD has a long way to go and that further work is necessary to fully understand, treat and hopefully, cure the disorder. Scientists hope that this can become a reality by combining all the pieces of the studies performed on humans and animals,

the biological nature of ADHD, and other similar

disorders. By breaking
 down the disorder into smaller parts and combining positive results, medical professionals hope to come up with the most effective treatments with which to successfully provide a remedy. Knowing and understanding the brain is key to providing the right approach, and treatment and possibly, preventing ADHD and other mental disorders.

Appendix